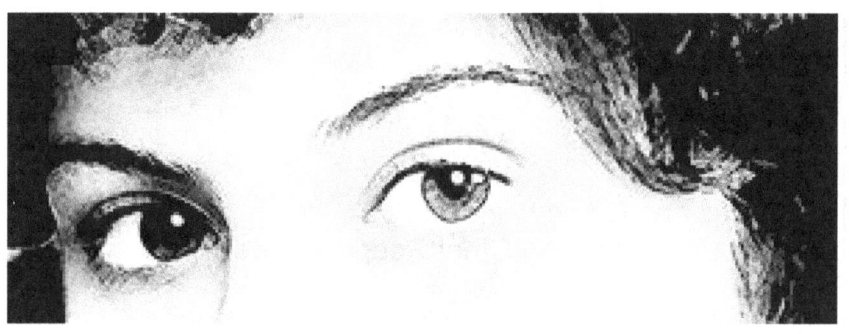

AUTISTIC

ME

TABLE OF CONTENTS

Page

For more information, visit **AutisticMe.org**

Author   - Amanda Hochfelder-Santi

Editing   - Evelyn Santi-Hochfelder, Psy.D.

                - Kelly Ann Santi

Illustrations   - Evelyn Santi-Hochfelder, Psy.D.

Artistic Editing - Peter Jimenez

                - Miguelangel Santimanzano

DEDICATION AND SPECIAL THANKS

This book is dedicated to some of the people that help me live a better life. I want to thank my mother for helping me put thoughts into words whenever I got stumped writing this book and for doing autistic exercises with me. I would also like to thank my dad Peter for always being available for anything I need and helping me with the artistic editing to make the book presentable. Thanks to my three dogs Peanut, Candy and Pipo for being so patient and never getting mad at me. Special thanks to Dr. Shelley Slapion-Foote for always being there for me and making me laugh. Thank you to Killian Oaks Academy for teaching, protecting me and making me feel important. To all the Tae Kwon Do staff, especially Mr. Isaacs, Mrs. Isaacs and Mr. Martin for their patience and encouragement which will help me get my black belt soon. To my Tio Teto, alias Miguelangel Santimanzano, for being so awesome in everything he does, using his amazing computer knowledge to make the book look pretty and fixing my electric scooter. Finally, to Tio Tony, Tia Kelly and my cousins Kaitlyn, Christina, Victoria and little Tony for loving me so much and always taking such good care of me. Tia Kelly also helped with the editing and found mistakes I had not caught with spell-check. Finally, this book is also dedicated to those autistics all over the world and their family members, who struggle like me every day to understand this complex world with hopes to finally fit in and live a better life.

SYNOPSIS

Autistic Me was written by 15 year old Amanda Hochfelder-Santi one year after becoming aware that she was autistic. It is an amazing view of the world as seen through the eyes of an autistic teenager. The book is geared toward other autistic individuals and their family members and educators who strive to help them fit in society and improve their quality of life and future outlook and success.

Amanda writes about some of the difficulties that she has encountered as an autistic teenager and explains in detail some of the exercises that have helped her overcome difficulties that she once faced. She focuses on important key factors that represent impediments for most people diagnosed within the spectrum. Included are eye contact, touch, social cues and communication. She also writes about repetitive behaviors, sudden noises, self-esteem, anxiety, routines and personal grooming.

Autistic Me contains valuable information which helps the reader understand the perspective, fear and difficulties faced by someone in the autism spectrum. Amanda provides suggestions and alternatives which have helped her better understand the world, social demands, rules and expectations. This is a valuable tool for autistic individuals and anyone that wants to help an autistic person live a better life.

INTRODUCTION

My name is Amanda. I am 15 years old. I found out last year that I am autistic.

There are a lot of things that I always wanted to do. Writing a book was one of them. When I started thinking about what type of book I wanted to write, I decided to write about being an autistic teenager. I know that there are a lot of people like doctors and scientists that do research and write about this. I am not a doctor or a scientist but I am autistic.

There are a lot of other kids like me out there who also have parents and other people that care about them. I thought that if I could write about the way I feel, the way I think and how I interpret things, it might be easier for people to understand us. Sharing exercises that have helped me deal with my autism might even help parents find other ways to help their kids.

There are different types and severity of autism. There is one type called Asperger's Syndrome and although it has some similarities and is on the same spectrum, it is not what I have. I am what they call high functioning autistic. I am very lucky to be high functioning because even though I am autistic, I can speak and do a lot of other things. There are a lot of autistic kids who do not speak and have a hard time communicating with other people. They are not able to tell anyone how they feel or how scared, happy or worried they may be. This makes me sad. Although I know that not all autistic kids think and feel the same way, there are a lot that are like me.

I wrote this book for two reasons. First, if you are autistic like me, you will see that you are not alone and maybe some of the exercises I do can help you as well. If you are not autistic, you will have the chance to see things from my point of view which might be similar to the point of view of an autistic person that you may know. This can help you get some ideas of how to help them overcome some of their fears and feel better about themselves.

My mother and I have created a number of exercises that help me deal with problem areas in my life. My mother is a doctor. She knows a lot of things and helps her patients use their minds to solve their problems. This is why she knows so much about autism and helps me do exercises. We call these "autistic exercises". These exercises do not come out of a book and were not suggested by my pediatrician.

The way that we create the exercises is by first pinpointing an area where I may be having problems with. I usually cannot tell which my problem areas are because being the way I am is normal for me. When my mother sees that there is something that we should work on, she brings it up to me. The funny thing is that there are many things today that I see that need attention but had not realized it in the past. Once we choose an area that I need to work on, then we create the exercise.

Each exercise is different because it is aimed to help me accomplish something that I may not be very good at. Sometimes we have to do a lot of trial and error. We devise the exercises together and then begin working on them. If there is no improvement after a number of attempts, then we have to make changes to it until we see some success. It is very frustrating to try something time after time and realize you are getting nowhere. Then after a few adjustments, sooner or later something clicks and it begins to work. I feel great when this happens.

I was 14 when I found out that I was autistic. That was just a year ago. At first, I got scared because I did not know what that meant. I remember that I was home watching a movie with my mother. There was someone in the movie that did a lot of the things that I do. Then, when I asked my mother about it, I remember she put the movie on pause and explained some things to me that I did not know. One of the things that she explained was that I was autistic.

I did not know what autism was. I got scared because it sounded strange. The first thing I asked my mother was if I was going to die. I was asking a lot of questions at the same time. She was trying to answer but more questions kept coming before she could finish her answers. Thinking about it now, my mouth was like a machine gun with all these bullets full of questions coming out really fast. My mother was trying to catch the bullets as fast as she could, put answers inside of them and send them back to me. She was not fast enough.

I wanted to know, Will I die soon? Is this contagious? How did I get this? Did you give this to me? Can I give it to my dogs? My mother was trying to calm me down and explained some things to me. She answered all my questions and then suggested we continue to see the movie.

There are some movies that are not very interesting but are made to teach you things. They are called educational movies. We watch these together and then, when they are finished, we talk about what we have learned. The movie that we were watching that day was one of those. My mom just wanted to make sure that I understood what the movie was about. I knew that as soon as the movie was over we were going to talk about being autistic some more. I kept watching the movie and the more I watched the more questions that came to my mind. I felt like a machine gun again with bullet-questions building up. Once the movie was over we talked about autism again. I did not understand everything my mother was explaining to me. Some things I did but others made no sense. I think I know more about it today but there are still some things that make no sense to me.

One of the most difficult things that I have to deal with is common sense. I looked up the meaning of common sense in the Webster's dictionary and definition states "normal native intelligence". Because it still did not make any sense, I looked up normal and its definition is "a typical or standard pattern". In other words, common sense is what most people that are somewhat intelligent would do in a specific situation. The problem is that autistics are not the majority of people in the world. In other words, we do not think like most people. It does not mean that we are not intelligent. It means that we see things differently and because of that we act in a different way. If most people in the world where autistic then we would be the ones with the common sense from the Webster's dictionary.

The most important thing that has made a change in my life is becoming aware of my autism. I always knew I was different but never understood why. Once I understood my diagnosis, many things became clear. I still have a long way to go but now I understand many more things than before. When you understand something, it is easier to do things. In my case, now when I do certain things it makes me feel better to know why I am doing them. The more I know about being autistic, the easier it is for me to either try to change the way I do things or not feel bad about things that happen.

I continue doing my exercises as often as I can and will probably do them for a very long time. Once I master an exercise and can do whatever the exercise was meant to do, I "graduate" from that particular one and look for a new one to work on. Most of the time, I practice different exercises throughout the day. That is why this book is going to be like a guide. I will share some of my experiences, tell you what has worked for me and will include some drawings to make my explanation more clear. It is possible that if you are autistic or know a high functioning autistic like me, that person may have some of the same difficulties that I have had. Maybe my experience may help them improve their life just like I have.

I have done some reading about autism. I agree with the doctors that I am an average high functioning autistic teenager. This is why sometimes I talk about myself using the words "us autistics" and "we". This does not mean that every autistic teenager out there sees or interprets all things the way I do. However, I think that most do.

There are some things that I have been working on that have helped me a lot. I know that I have improved a lot this past year. I have worked very hard on a number of things and it has been worth it. Everyone around me including my family, parents of my friends and my teachers say that this is true. It can be very hard and frustrating sometimes when something sets me back or when it seems that something is not working. This was especially true at the beginning when I found out I was autistic. Looking back now, I know that all it took was to be successful in any of the things I tried to accomplish. That gave me the strength to keep going and I feel that I have gone a really long way. There are a lot of things that I still need to work on but I only write about the ones that I feel have been the most difficult ones for me.

EYE CONTACT

Most people look at each other when they are having a conversation. It is polite to look at the person that you are speaking to because it lets them know that you are listening.
Looking into someone's eyes can make us feel uncomfortable and scared. For some reason that I cannot yet understand, we feel "threatened" when we stare into a person's eyes, especially if the face belongs to a stranger. For this reason, most autistics avoid eye contact while having a conversation. However, we do look at the person when we think that they are not aware of it. Many times, we can be seen as rude or thought not be interested in the conversation. However, that is not the case. It is very difficult to have a conversation with a person while you are feeling threatened, scared or concerned.

I used to have a hard time when someone looked at me or I needed to look at someone in the face. I would be concerned about what they would be thinking rather than about what they were saying. I used to feel scared and sometimes threatened. Many questions would come to my mind such as: "Are they looking to hurt me?" or "Why am I being stared at?" I would also think that if I was caught staring at someone they would become upset. I would be too busy thinking about all these questions instead of paying attention to what they were saying. Of course, when it was my turn to participate I would not know what to say because I had not paid attention to the conversation.

man

Amanda

This used to happen to me mostly with strangers. Most of the time, I do not have a problem looking at people that I know. This used to happen to me not only with people but with pictures as well. If I saw a picture of someone I did not know I would try to avoid staring at the eyes. This may make no sense to some people. I think about it and it really does not make any sense to me. A picture can't hurt you. However, there is no logic to being autistic.

I like to make comparisons and give examples because I feel that this makes it easier for other people to understand me. There are a lot of people that do not like snakes. They have a hard time looking at them even if it's in a picture. They sense something threatening about the image and find it very hard to ignore. I want to compare what we experience when we look into somebody's eyes to the feeling of people who are afraid of snakes may feel when they look at them. It is probably the same feeling that we get when we look into the eyes of a person either live or in a picture. Of course, we feel a bigger threat when the person is in front of us. The funny thing is that I love snakes. I think they are beautiful and can stare at them in both pictures and real life. I even like to hold them and pet them when I know they are not poisonous but snakes are not people. Most of them will not hurt you if you leave them alone. Some people are not so kind. For this reason I sometimes still wonder what someone is thinking about when they look at me.

The first exercise that I want to share has to do with eye contact. I started working on this by staring at my eyes in the mirror. I know my face and luckily I am not afraid of it. However, it was important to begin the exercise by feeling a stare without being threatened, even if it was my own. That was easy. When I felt comfortable staring in the mirror then my family helped by practicing with me. We made it into a game where we would have short conversations and the idea was to look at the other person most of the time while they were speaking. At the beginning I had a hard time looking into their eyes so I would stare at them in between the eyebrows. I started doing this for 15 seconds at a time. Once I felt comfortable, I was able to go to the next step and take turns looking at the person at each eye for a few seconds at a time while we kept having our conversation. I went from having 15 second conversations to 30 second conversations and so on.

I have described this in a few sentences but it took me some time to be able to do this. It took me at least 30 days to practice with close family members like my mother, my favorite cousin Christina… even my dogs. My dogs were very easy to do and never a problem. Most of the times that I stared at them, they would come close to me wagging their tails and trying to lick me on the face. I guess I always knew that I am their boss and they were not going to hurt me. That made this exercise easy to do with them.

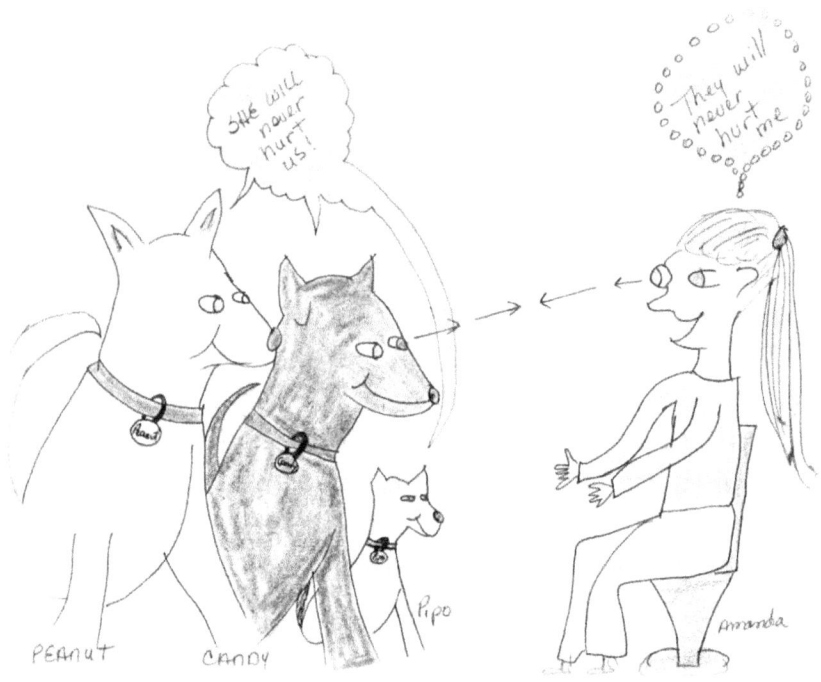

Once I felt I mastered the visual contact with people that I knew, I started performing the exercise with strangers without their knowledge. I would try it with the lady at the cash register at the supermarket, the bank teller, and other people that appeared suddenly. I would start with simple things like saying good morning or thanking them when they finished taking care of us. Sometimes I would ask them for the time. It was hard at the beginning but I always remembered that this was part of an exercise. Little by little I started feeling more confident when I spoke to strangers. Today, I am able to have short conversations with better eye contact. I have also learned to nod my head in agreement or disagreement and include "yes, no and I see" when I feel it is appropriate. This lets the other person know that I am paying attention and that I understand what they are telling me. I have noticed that lately people enjoy having conversations with me a lot more than before.

I have to admit that up to now I have always done these exercises when I am in the company of a family member. I feel a lot better knowing that there is someone there that can help me in case something goes wrong. You never know when somebody may be in a bad mood and may snap at you. It worries me not knowing what to do if that would happen.

My next step is to initiate and practice the exercises alone without anyone guiding me. I feel that the worst has already passed. A year ago I could barely have a simple conversation with someone that I knew well. My visual contact has improved tremendously this past year. However, I must continue practicing the because I have realized that the more I practice, the more I improve and the better I feel.

Television has helped me a lot. I can watch how people act with each other and how they use their eyes. Eyes say a lot about how someone is feeling. I have learned to read surprise, sadness, fear and happiness. I still have a hard time with a sneaky stare because it usually comes with a smile and that can confuse me. The good thing about television is that I can stare as long as I want, rewind and fast forward and do not have to worry about anyone becoming uncomfortable or upset because I am watching them.

My eye contact has improved a lot this past year. I know that I should continue working on this because there are still some times that I feel uncomfortable. Today, I am able to have longer conversations with better eye contact. I have noticed that people enjoy having conversations with me more than before because they believe that I am paying attention to what they are saying.

TOUCH

Most autistic kids do not like to be touched. Being touched is like being stared at but it feels even more threatening. The same way that we wonder why somebody is looking at us we also wonder why someone is touching us.

One of the things I have learned through exercises and watching movies is that a lot of people touch each other as part of their conversation. They are communicating through their bodies. However, here is where common sense comes in again and this is one of the areas where we have a lot of difficulty. We can misinterpret the meaning of the touch. Since most of us autistics tend to communicate and interpret things differently than most people, our common sense does not help much when we try to interpret somebody's reason for touching us. Someone may touch you to get your attention, to show you that they love you, to comfort you or to hurt you.

In order for me to have a successful conversation with someone, there are a lot of steps that I have to follow. If I am trying to integrate my visual and physical contact in the conversation, I can use a lot of mental energy in just a few seconds. There are lots of things happening in my mind at the same time to which I have to pay attention to and find its meaning as soon as possible. This is so that I can understand and participate in the conversation in a logical way.

First I have to figure out if there is any type of threat going on. Some people may touch you just to get your attention. Other people make touch you because they are used to touching others while they speak but it may mean nothing. Other people may touch you to threaten or hurt you.

The problem is that it's not just the touch that we have to understand. We have to react to many different things like who is touching us, how hard or soft is their touch and what is their tone of voice like. It is also important to look at their face in order to understand the touch. If they are smiling it means something different than if they look angry. If you know the person that is touching you, it is easier to react. There are a lot of things to try and put together very quickly to react in an appropriate way. There is so much to keep in mind and very little time to react. For this reason touch is very difficult for most autistics. I am very proud to say that I have improved a lot in this area. It has been a very difficult year but all my hard work has paid off.

Doing exercises helped my eye contact. Other exercises having to do with touch also helped me. At the beginning, all the exercises I did were with people that knew that this was a form of training for me. This made it easier because I felt I was somewhat in control and could stop at any time. I went from having a conversation with someone to continuing the conversation while I touched their shoulder or their hair. When they did the same I did not feel threatened. This works well with family members or close friends. However, it is more difficult with people that you are not familiar with. There are people that are not autistic that do not like to be touched by strangers. I have learned that unless you are a doctor or someone else that needs to touch people as part of your job, you should not touch anyone. However, there are many people who get very close and touch you as part of their conversation. For this reason, even if I do not touch strangers I needed to learn to react to someone's touch and decide if they are friendly or not. Once I felt comfortable with my touching exercises, I felt it was time to move on to something more challenging.

I enrolled in a Tae Kwon Do school. I knew this was going to be a huge challenge. I thought about it for weeks before making up my mind. At that time, I had known I was autistic for about six months. I had already been working on my eye contact as well as my touch. I went to the school a few times to see the other kids while they were in class before I started. I became familiar with the instructor's faces, the sounds, and some of the routines. I noticed some of the things that were done like how the students came into the school and placed their attendance card on a specific slot. Then they would remove their shoes, bow to enter the Tae Kwon Do area and put their things away. This seemed very easy because it was always the same routine. I was a little concerned about what came after. The teacher would tell the students to do certain exercises but they were not always the same ones. Sometimes they would kick and sometimes they would punch. The problem is that not all the kicks were the same and neither were the punches. What I thought would be the hardest part was sparring. This is when students put on their protective gear and fight each other. I knew this was going to be the biggest challenge so far. I was right.

I am very lucky to have found this school. The instructors and junior instructors are very nice. I was concerned that they were not going to like me because I did not know what to do. I was wrong. Mr. and Mrs. Isaacs are the owners of the school and also teach. They are very patient with me. Mr. Martin is very cool and tough. He takes time off his job and goes to school early sometimes to help me with some of my moves and spars with me. Even with all this help, it was very difficult.

I had to meet a lot of students and keep up with them. I did the exercises and practiced the moves I was told.

The toughest thing was when we had to spar with each other. Many times I cried quietly but never stopped sparring until class was over. Even though I knew it was part of class I did not like it when I got hit. They never hurt me when they hit me but they were touching me. My body did not feel pain but my mind was going crazy. To make matters worse, they would stare at me to see where to hit and then hit me again. I had to deal with the two most difficult things for me which were touching and staring. I had to look at them so that I could see where they were going to hit me and then try to block them. This involved more staring and touching. I really had a hard time because I would try to hit back without looking at them. I probably looked like a blind person trying to hit a baseball. At the same time I was afraid they would get mad at me if I hit them back. I knew I was supposed to but was afraid to do it.

Somehow, I felt okay if I was fighting an instructor. This is because they would talk to me and tell me what to do as they were fighting me. That way I knew it was okay to fight back and they would not be upset. The problem was that most of the time I would be fighting another student. It is difficult to explain how I felt at the time. I was scared, confused and frustrated. I knew what to do but could not bring myself to do it right. This is why I cried many times but I always went back. I had decided that I was going to do this because I wanted a black belt. I am still working on it.

I am proud to say that I only miss Tae Kwon Do when I have too much homework and cannot make it on time. I try to make it every day because I know that the more I go the better I will become. I would like to share a success story so that it will be easier to understand how the exercises have helped me.

About six months ago, Mr. Martin told me about a Tae Kwon Do Tournament coming up in the state of Florida. I would have to compete against other kids from other schools in two different categories. The first category was in form. This one is not so bad because students get to do their forms in front of judges and they do not have to touch or look at each other. The second category was sparring. I was worried about this one because I had to fight someone that I did not know. I was offered to compete in the special category. This is for kids my age who have some type of disability. I probably would have done better in this special category but I thought that my classmates would laugh at me. I decided to go to the tournament and compete in the regular category.

The week before the tournament was very hard for me. I kept thinking about what would happen. We had to go very far from our house to a place I did not know. I was going to compete with people I did not know and I was probably going to get beat up by strangers. I was right but I am glad.

When we got to the tournament, I saw some of the students from my school competing in other areas. When it was my turn, some of those students came over to my area and were cheering for me. I felt very good although I was very nervous. I had never had so many people cheering for me. I remember that they were yelling out my name…

"Amanda...Amanda…Go, Amanda, Go! Good job, Amanda!!!" At the end, my form was not the best but I got second place in sparring. It came with a beautiful medal around my neck. My mother cried but said she was happy. This successful event showed me how good my autistic exercises were working. This is why I can never practice them too much.

SOCIAL CUES AND COMMUNICATION

This is probably the most difficult area for us to deal with. I am still working on this area and I find it very challenging.

There are different ways that people communicate with each other. They can speak, or they can do body movements. People with autism say what they mean, exactly the way they feel it. If I am hungry I say: "I am hungry". It sounds logical for me to say what I feel when I feel it. However, I have found out that it is not socially acceptable to do this in many situations. This confuses me and many times makes me feel unsure of what to do.

Dealing with people that I know is usually not a problem for me. This is because I am already familiar with the person and most of the time I can tell what they mean, how they are feeling and what they are about to do. Dealing with a stranger is more difficult. If people communicated using language only, then it would be easier to know what they mean. However, I have to interpret what they are saying, their facial expression, body movements and tone of voice. Here are two different meanings to a similar picture: The first one is someone tapping you softly on the shoulder, with a smile on their face and a singing tone of voice, telling you that they are happy because you ate all the cookies.

The second one is someone tapping you hard on the shoulder with a frown on their face and a rough tone of voice telling you that they are happy because you ate all the cookies.

The first example matches all around but the second one is sending different signals. This is what people call sarcasm.

These examples happen every day all the time. The problem is that they do not always happen the same exact way. When speaking to a stranger I pay attention to everything they do in order to figure out what they are trying to tell me. Sometimes it's very difficult to do this. If their face does not match their words, tone of voice and other body language then I will be confused. In most cases you only have a second or two before it's your turn to speak. It is very difficult to respond to someone when you are not sure what they are telling you. There have been times where I was asked something but did not answer because I was not sure what I was being asked or told. This makes me feel bad because people may think I am ignoring them or just being rude because I may not answer right away. In most cases, that is not the case.

Most autistic people like me like patterns because we like to know what is coming next. It makes me feel good to know what is going to happen because I feel that I have some control over the matter. If I ask a question about when something is going to happen I do not like to get "soon" for an answer. "Soon" does not give me an answer to my question. If the answer I am given is "in one year" then I would be happy because I know that it means exactly 365 days and tomorrow will be 364, the next day would be 363 and so on until there would be no more days left. Unfortunately, these answers that most people call "concrete" are not used most of the time.

Everyone acts in a different way, with a different tone of voice, different expressions on their face and so on. I will never be able to know exactly how everyone is going to act or what they are going to say. For this to happen, I would have to meet every person in the world and memorize millions and millions of different combinations and possible patterns. Then, I would have to be able to analyze all the patterns and decide which one someone is using at that time, all within a second or two so that I have enough time to understand what they mean and give them a right answer. I cannot do this. However, there are other things that I can do to improve my understanding of social cues and communication.

First impressions are very important. If people like you, there is a bigger chance that they will be patient with you. It is still hard for me to approach a stranger but when I do I try to put a smile on my face. This is hard because I have to think about it and plan it. Most people that are not autistic do not have to plan this because they do it without thinking. The reason I use a smile is because I have learned that most people do not like to feel threatened and if they are approached by someone that is smiling they may react better. This does not always work but it helps most of the time. This exercise has taken me a lot of work. Remember that autistic people say and do things exactly the way they feel. Our common sense works differently than people who are not autistic.

Some time ago, it did not make any sense to approach someone with a smile on my face unless I was thinking about something that made me smile. Today this has changed because I understand a little better that a smile can take you a long way and I try to use it to ease the initial impact when I meet somebody for the first time. My smile may look forced because I am forcing a smile at the same time that I am reviewing in my head what I am going to say, how I'm going to say it and at the same time, I am trying to predict out how the stranger is going to react. Just like when someone wants to take your picture and they ask you to smile. I have seen pictures of people that were forcing their smile and it reminds me of me when I do mine.

Amanda

Photographer

The mirror has helped me a lot. I practice looking at my face while I smile. This helps me see how I look like with a smile on my face. I practice with my family. I practice having conversations with them and at the same time I observe their smiles when they speak to me. The hardest part is, not knowing when to stop. Having a conversation with someone for more than one minute with a smile on my face is hard to do. I practice turning the smile on and off throughout the conversation. I also do this exercise while I am watching movies. I usually record movies I like so that I am able to choose 5 minutes from the movie where I can rewind over and over and see how people use their smiles during their conversation.

The movies have helped me a lot. I can watch parts over and over and the characters are not aware that I am watching them. This way is better than doing it while you watch strangers talk to each other because sometimes they don't like it when you stare at them. I have noticed that there are people that even though may not be autistic, they can feel uncomfortable when they are having a conversation and realize that another person is observing them. By watching the recorded movies, I can see the behavior and interaction of people without bothering anyone.

Something to keep in mind is that a smile is not always appropriate. I pay close attention to the topic of the conversation and the other person's face. If someone is talking about something bad that happened to them, I have to be careful not to put a smile on. In that case it is better to skip the smile and try and read the face of the other person. If they are sad, it may work to copy their face. But be careful that they don't think you are mocking them. It is tricky for me to deal with someone that is angry or surprised.

Some of the movies that I have recorded to do exercises with show people who are very angry. I have noticed that when two people that are having a conversation are angry it usually ends up in an argument or fight. It is also difficult to have a conversation with someone that is very sad. If I put on a straight face they may think I don't care about their problem. If I put on an angry face, they may think I am upset at them for being sad. If I put on a sad face they may end up crying even more. All these different possibilities go through my mind when I have conversations with other people. There are so many things to keep in mind that sometimes it is hard to concentrate on the conversation.

All of these things and many more go through my mind when I interact with people. There are lots of things that we have to keep in mind in order to make sure that we understand everything correctly. I only mention here the most obvious ones, which I think are the basis of many other factors which are very important in social communication. There are obviously so many things to keep in mind at the same time that it makes it harder to concentrate in what is going on. However, I believe that I am getting better at this with all the practice that I am doing.

EMPATHY: UNDERSTANDING OTHER PEOPLE'S FEELINGS

Understanding feelings of others may be hard for an autistic person because of our difficulty in understanding how people react. Remember that we have a difficult time with social cues and communication. Therefore, the ability to understand how others may feel may be blocked.

We can improve our understanding of other people's feelings if we are reminded of them frequently. This is an exercise that I cannot do alone. The help of a second person is needed for this exercise. That person needs to be very familiar with the autistic individual and has to be available on a regular basis so that the exercises can be performed as frequently as possible.

In my case, it helps me a lot to be reminded of other people's feelings. My exercise partner helps me understand how someone may feel by teaching me how to place myself in someone else's shoes. Sometimes it is hard for me to understand somebody else's situation and this is where my partner comes in. There are stories, comparisons and examples that help me as long as they are told in a concrete and specific way and include me as the main character. This way, I can visualize a specific scenario.

My partner begins telling me a story about how there used to be a girl called Amanda who was going through a particular situation and helps me visualize the scenario and feelings of the girl in the story. This way, it is easier for me to understand happiness, sadness, concerns and fears that the girl may be having. Sometimes it is difficult but it works for me most of the time. It is important to have a good patient partner that knows the autistic person very well. The examples that are given to help us visualize cannot be threatening. Remember that the autistic person can perceive a statement as a fact. When giving us an example, it needs to be clear that it is just an example which may help us better understand a particular situation. It is important that we understand that the example is not something that is going to happen to us in the future.

An example will help me explain this better. About a year ago, my mother was driving around our neighborhood and saw a little dog close to our house. She told me that a lady was chasing him away with a broom from her driveway. The dog looked scared and was walking away slowly.

My mother pulled over and asked the lady if that was her dog or if he was lost. The lady explained that his name was Pipo and it was her dog but she did not want him anymore and told my mother that she could take him if she wanted him. When I got home from school, the dog was home and my mother told me the story of how the dog got there. She told me she was going to try and find a home for him since we already had two other dogs but that never happened because he is still with us.

At the beginning, I did not like him much. My mother was very nice to him and played with him a lot. It made me feel sad. He was always following her around and playing with her. When we were watching television, he would come on the couch and sit next to her so that she could pet him. I remember feeling upset and would move him from the couch and sit next to my mother. Then I would lay my head on her legs so that she could stroke my hair. He would wait until I moved and would jump on the couch again, taking my space. When he would see that I was coming back, he would jump off the couch. I was upset because he never came to me so that I could rub his head or never sat next to me to watch television. I told my mother I wanted him to go to another house.

My mother and I had to spend some time working on exercises to help me understand other people's feelings. Up to this time, my mother had been using some examples and I would understand a little here and there but not all of it. However, I think that when she used examples with the dog, it was the first time that I really understood better about other's feelings. Dogs are not people but they have feelings. The easy thing about dogs is that they act the way they feel, just like autistic people do. If they are sad or happy, you know. They do not use strange social cues, double meanings or sarcasm. Best of all, they always forgive you if you make a mistake and they always know when you are sad and try to make you happy.

The example my mother used was about a little girl called Amanda. She did not have a home or anyone to care of her.

She was lost in a strange place, and was afraid, cold and hungry. At night, she found shelter in some shrubs but could not sleep because she was very afraid of all the strange noises around her.

She noticed that there were a couple of rats close by that were staring at her and were probably waiting for Amanda to fall asleep so that they could eat her. They were even holding a fork and knife.

At that moment, a lady who was taking a night stroll saw the little girl hiding in the bushes. She realized that the little girl was lost and was afraid. The lady also noticed that there were rats waiting for the right moment to attack. The lady took Amanda's hands and spoke to her softly. She asked her if she would like to go to her house and live with her. Amanda happily accepted. When they got to the house, the lady fixed her a nice warm bath and gave her clean clothes. Then they ate a delicious dinner and finally sat on the sofa together to watch a movie. Amanda felt so happy and so protected that she would place her head her new owners' lap while the lady caressed her hair. The lady loved and protected Amanda from that moment on.

My mother would ask me how I thought Amanda would feel towards the lady and then I understood. At the beginning I was scared and upset because I could picture me sleeping under bushes, being cold, hungry, dirty and afraid. I could even picture rats looking at me waiting for me to fall asleep so they could eat me. My mother kept on reminding me that it was a story whenever she would notice that I was getting upset. She reminded me many times until I did not have to be reminded any more. I finally understood how the girl felt. If someone rescued me, I would sit next to them on the couch too. I would follow them around all the time to make sure they do not go away and leave me. It would make me sad if someone moved me away from the couch but the moment that the person who moved me leaves, I would jump right back next to the lady because I would want that person to love me all the time.

First, I was happy that I finally understood. Then, I was sad that I had been so mean to the dog. I stopped calling him dog and began to call him Pipo. That is the name his previous owner had given him. My mother had a good point. I would not like it if everyone called me "girl". Then I was surprised. Right after I started calling him by his name, he started to follow me around. He would let me pet him and he would sometimes sit on the couch next to me. Now he lays his head on my lap and wags his tail. We take him in the car every morning to drop me off at school and to pick me up in the afternoon. He goes crazy when he spots me among the kids at school. I hear him barking from far away and I can tell that I have a big smile on my face. That smile I do not have to practice because it comes on its own. I am so glad that Pipo lives with us.

This exercise cannot be done alone. Someone else has to notice a situation that can be used to help us learn and be able to create a good non-threatening example. That person needs to be very patient and willing to repeat the exercise as many times as are needed changing some of the facts of the story until they "click" the right way. It took me a long time to find an example that helped me understand how other people may feel. My mother did this type of exercise with me many times before and I would understand a little here and there. I learned something from all of them but I think the Pipo story was the best so far. I do these exercises as often as possible. I usually do not bring them up but when I am asked to do a new one, I do not get as upset as I used to because I am seeing how they are helping me.

Exercises are not the only way to improve on empathy. Understanding how other people feel can improve by watching other people, either in real life or in movies. I watched a movie called ET. It was about an alien that came to Earth with his parents and got lost. A family found him and helped him find his parents and return to his planet. This is a very old movie but my mother rented it after we got Pipo to help me understand how Pipo felt. Just like Pipo, ET was scared, alone and hungry. He found a boy who loved him and helped him. Then ET was not scared anymore and he loved the family that had helped him.

The good thing about watching movies at home is that I can rewind a scene as many times as I want so that I can see the expression on people's faces. This helps me understand things like facial expressions when showing fear, surprise and excitement. I can also pause and ask questions about something that I do not understand. You cannot do this at the movie theater because the movie cannot be paused and the other people can become upset if you talk too much.

PICTURES

Understanding is easier for me if I can picture or feel what I am being told. Many autistic kids like me think in pictures some or most of the time. I like watching cartoons. Many times that I see pictures in my head they come in the form of a cartoon drawing. When I hear someone speak my mind begins to create pictures that show what the person is saying.

One time, a classmate told me that she was in a bad mood. She said that she was so hungry that she could eat a horse. My mind started creating a lot of pictures of what she was saying. I imagined at least 100 different pictures in my head almost at the same time. All of them showed her with an upset face. In some of the pictures her eyes were big and popping out and in others they were closed. Some of the faces were green, black or red. In some of the pictures her mouth was open with her tongue sticking out and in others it was close. Many times my images have different sounds, like a lion's roar. All these images would come to my mind almost at the same time and I could see my classmate in different ways with a napkin tied around her neck and a fork and knife on her hands chasing a scared horse in the middle of a farm. I remember all the different types of horses that I imagined and they were all of different colors and sizes. Of course, they all made different sounds as they were running away from my friends.

Everyone has been hungry at some point. Being in a bad mood because you are hungry may seem normal so agreeing with the person and talking about how you feel when you are hungry maybe a normal way of continuing with the conversation. But first, I have to make sure that I understand what they are telling me.

The reason why I think I imagine all of these pictures in my head is because I'm trying to visualize what I am being told. I imagine so many pictures because I try to find the one specific one that the person may be referring to. This can be very frustrating because many times I am not sure of which one they are talking about.

Many autistics tend to do repetitive behaviors and can become easily obsessed with a topic. I will talk about this in more detail later on. At the moment I just want to mention that once I get a thought or picture in my head it is hard to let it go. The picturing situation has created problems for me in the past. Because of the great amount of pictures that pop into my head when I try to understand what I am being told, there have been many times where funny pictures have made me laugh. I have spoken to people who are angry or sad and suddenly burst into a laughter that I cannot control. This has made some people upset or disappointed at my behavior. They thought I was making fun of them. I was not. If I could have brought them into my mind and let them see the pictures I was watching they would probably have laughed as well but this cannot be.

Everyone has sudden thoughts or pictures that come to their mind. You may be watching television or watching dogs play and have a thought pop in your mind. This happens to autistic people as well. A non-autistic person may have an easier time getting rid of the thought by doing something else. Due to my tendency for repetitive behaviors and obsessions, it is very hard to get rid of a thought that is distracting me or that may come to my mind at a bad moment. It may cause problems because of bad timing. This happened to me a few months back.

I was in Tae Kwon Do class a couple months ago. The instructors were Mr. and Mrs. Isaacs, and Mr. Martin. I respect them a lot. We were all practicing our kicks and forms. All of a sudden one of my classmates made a strange sound after he got kicked. It sounded like the same type of sound that a scared alien would make. All of a sudden I pictured everyone in class with an alien head. It was hilarious. Their heads where huge! They looked like the alien from the movie ET. The bodies were the normal student bodies but everyone had an alien head with the same hairdo as the students. My teacher, Mr. Isaacs, shaves his head. His alien head had no hair. I thought it was hilarious to see all these aliens in Tae Kwon Do uniforms practicing their moves.

I felt I was going to crack up so I pressed my lips together really hard. A whole wall in class is a mirror. I kept on pressing my lips together as hard as I could. When I looked at the mirror, because of the reflection, there were twice as many alien heads in class. That was it. I burst into a laughter that I thought I could not stop. All of a sudden I noticed that Mr. Isaacs was looking at me. I felt horrible. He is a very important person and I did not want to disappoint him. I turned around and continued to practice my moves but all I could see in my head were pictures of Mr. Isaacs' blue eyes looking at me. I looked at the mirror and he was not looking at me anymore. However, my mind kept creating picture after picture after picture of Mr. Isaacs' face.

I learned two very important things from my alien experience. Even though I have obsessive thoughts, something that is important or serious to me can stop them. Mr. Isaacs has been good to me and the thought of him not liking me stopped the alien thoughts I was having.

The first thing I learned was that I can stop an obsessive thought or idea as long as I can think of a negative consequence to having that thought at the time. Whenever I get inappropriate thoughts at Tae Kwon Do, I remember how Mr. Isaacs could dislike me and the funny thoughts usually go away quick. I am still working on this.

The second thing I learned was that sometimes I am obsessed with things that are not really happening. Thinking about it over and over, I don't think that Mr. Isaacs noticed I was laughing. He is always looking at all the students and maybe I just happened to look at him at the same time he was glancing over in my direction. I am not sure. All I know is that the fear of him being upset at me made all the aliens vanish into space really fast.

ROUTINE

Autistic people usually do not like change. A change in routine can be very stressful. Having control over what is going to happen next allows me to predict outcomes. Knowing what an outcome will be makes me feel relaxed. Unfortunately, I do not always have control over things. I can control everyday activities like mealtimes, showering, getting dressed or going to bed. However, there are situations that are difficult to control such as weather and other people's reactions. The point is to understand how autistics react to situations that they have no control over compared to non-autistics.

Individuals who are not in the autistic spectrum have a better ability to accept changes. If a person was planning to go to the beach but it starts to rain, he may choose to go to the movies instead. An autistic person is not so flexible. I have been working on exercises to get better at dealing with changes and I feel they are working very well. Before I began my exercises, I had a lot more frustrations than I do today.

For example, in the past, I had planned a day at the beach and it started to rain. My whole day was ruined because it was more difficult for me to deal with change. This is where my need to control and predict outcomes comes in.

I have been going to the same beach for a long time so I am very familiar with it. I used to spend the previous days planning the day at the beach. I would plan ahead of time and decide which bathing suit to wear, which sunscreen to take, what food to bring, the towel… Even the spot I was going to sit on! Any little change would upset me because I already had a mental picture of the whole plan and once the picture was completed and I hit "save", I could not make any changes to it. If I got to the beach and my spot was taken, I would not want to sit anywhere else. I would sit as close as possible to the people who took my spot and just wait. Sometimes they left maybe because they did not like me being so close or because they had been there for a long time. Then, I was finally happy. If I ran out of sunscreen, I would not want to apply from a different bottle. If it started to rain, I would want to stay there, under the rain, waiting for it to stop. My next couple of days would be ruined and I would not want to go to the beach for a while after that.

It is very difficult or impossible to control certain things that affect me. All I can do is work on those things that I can control. The exercises I do to learn to cope with changes seem simple but they are very stressful, especially at the beginning. Here is one example of how I started working on changes.

The first thing I did was find something that I could control to use for my new exercise. I decided to use mealtimes with all the routine and patterns around it. A typical meal time for me meant sitting on the same chair, using the same plate and cup, and having my meal divided into sections such as squares, which I would eat in a specific order. First all the meat, followed by all of the side dish. If there was bread, it would be eaten first.

My exercise was to make little changes on each meal. I know my own routine. I remember specifically the order in which I do things. Knowing that I am trying to change my order and routine makes me a little anxious but I don't feel too nervous since I always remember that I can stop the exercise any moment I wish. This is because once again I feel I have certain control over what is going on. I think that my exercises would not work if at any time I would feel that I cannot stop them.

I started my routine exercises by changing the way in which I cut the meat. I would only cut the piece that I was going to take to my mouth and did not cut it in the shape of a square. I did not change anything else for that meal time. I remember it took me six meals to feel comfortable enough to go to the next step.

The second step was changing the order in which I ate what I had in my plate. This was much harder for me because there were more steps involved. I know what I was doing but it made no sense to my mind to change my routine. It's as if my hand already knew what my mouth wanted and would aim for it. I guess this is like telling someone else that they have to eat their dessert first. At any rate, I was finally able to mix in a piece of meat with some of the side dish in the same mouthful. I was also able to take bites of the bread throughout the meal and not eat it first like I used to. The truth is that doing things in this order still does not make sense to me. However, it helps me to remember that I am trying to learn to do things the same way that most people do them. This way, it'll be easier for me to behave as expected when I am in a social setting.

The third step was eating on a different plate other than the one that I was used to. I kept my favorite cup. This was also hard to do at the beginning. Suddenly, I realized that all the anxiety that I was feeling because of the new plate, was making me not to think so much on the fact that I was not eating in the order that I wanted to or that I had not cut the meat into squares. I was just focusing on the new plate and everything else was secondary, but still there.

The fourth step consisted on sitting at a different place on the table each meal. The chair was never a problem for me. What did bother me was changing places at the table. I had my favorite spot and would not allow anyone else to sit there. Once I had completed steps one and two and three, then I started changing spots. I would pick a spot for Monday, a different one for Tuesday, and so on. Today, I am able to sit anywhere on the table. The truth is that I still have a favorite spot and usually sit there. However, if I am asked to change places or if we have company for dinner, it does not bother me so much to do so.

None of these exercises can be forced. The support of people around us is very important but if we are not interested or do not understand what the purpose is, the exercise would most likely not work. These exercises take up a lot of time. The steps have to be taken slowly and only go to the next one after the previous one has been mastered.

All of these behaviors are learned and do not just happen on their own. What I keep in mind is that even if the exercises seem strange to me, the behaviors that I am trying to learn are expected by most people. I have no other choice but to learn them if I want to fit in. Even after I master an exercise, I have the same tendencies. If I could choose, or if I knew that no one can see me, I like it better when I cut my food in squares or when I eat in the order that I prefer. The purpose of the exercises is not to change the way I am as I don't believe that that can be done. It is like if someone told me that I could no longer like chocolate. The purpose is to learn to make certain changes so that when I am with people that are not like me, I can have a positive interaction without seeming weird. I no longer question if what I am learning makes sense or not. I just try to make the changes without spending the rest of the day feeling upset by what I did. Remembering that I am doing an exercise helps me deal and accept the change.

At the end of the day I share my feelings with my family and we talk about what my reaction was and if I was able to function correctly the rest of the day.

Once I was able to cope with simple changes, such as meals, I graduated to other exercises. Some were harder than others. They are all hard at the beginning but become easier with time. Some of the easier things that I worked on making changes to were the route to school, my hairdo, what I take for school lunch and which homework subject to work on first. I still have a hard time dealing with changes that disappoint me. Having to cancel a fun trip is very hard but I think that everyone can be disappointed at cancelling something fun. That is not part of being autistic. That is part of being a person. Today, I am proud to say that I have very few problems dealing with change. I can be disappointed and become sad or angry but I know that this is normal and that I function better when it comes to coping with change.

REPETITIVE BEHAVIORS:

I mentioned how people with autism like to predict and feel in control when they know what is going to happen next. For this reason, doing repetitive behaviors feels good and relaxing. When I draw a picture over and over, hum the same tune or twirl in circles, it makes me feel good. I am in control of what I am doing, how many times I do it, and I know ahead of time what the outcome is going to be. It also helps me burn energy. I think that this is a typical pattern of autistic people like me.

I have observed people a lot. Most of the exercises I do include observing other people so that I can learn how other people behave and what their reactions are. I have observed that people who are not autistic have repetitive movements too. Most of the time, they do these movements to feel relaxed... just like me. I have seen people humming at the supermarket, drawing patterns on a paper at the bank and parents shaking their knees for a long time while sitting down watching their kids during Tae Kwon Do class. By observing people I realized that everyone makes these movements at some point. The problem is knowing when it is appropriate to make them and to be able to stop when the timing is wrong. Autistic people like me have a hard time telling when our timing is off. It usually takes someone else bringing it to our attention for us to realize and stop. However, if I am doing something that calms me down, it is probably because I am nervous. If someone lets me know that what I am doing is inappropriate, I may become more nervous and may continue doing that inappropriate behavior even more. It is not something I do to bother anyone. I just may not be able to stop unless I quickly find another way to calm down.

Autistic kids like me have a hard time making changes and this is true even more when we are put on the spot or under pressure. I will share an example of something that happened to me a while back.

I went to the park with my parents. It was full of kids about my age so I was a little intimidated. My mother encouraged me to climb onto a huge spider web-like structure that goes in circles when the kids spin it. I climbed all the way to the top with other kids and it felt very good to sit there and go in circles. All of the sudden a lady stood in front of the structure and yelled at me. The kids stopped spinning the structure. She said something about taking turns spinning the web. I froze and did not know what to do. I was happily spinning around, feeling good and not bothering anyone. All of the sudden there was a grownup yelling at me and all the kids were staring at me… I was so shocked that I could not move an inch. All of the sudden, my mother jumped out of nowhere like a lion chasing a zebra. Even though she was yelling at the lady, I could not understand anything she was saying. I was too scared and it just seemed that she was roaring. The lady took her daughter and ran away. Judging by the look on her face, I think she also thought my mother was a lion. Right after that, my mother told me and all the kids that were on the structure to hold onto real tight while she took turns spinning the structure with the other kids.

The spinning made feel much better and all the kids were very nice. I remember that time because I froze and wish I was invisible. I was in the middle of feeling good and relaxed and someone interrupted me in a mean way. It felt like being at the beach, lying on the sand with your eyes closed, listening to the seagulls and all of the sudden it becomes pitch black and there are a thousand fireworks exploding one foot away from your ears. It can be very scary.

It is difficult or impossible to control some things, like what happened to me at the park. I had no control over the lady that yelled at me. I wanted to spin the web because you go in circles and I love that but I was too shy to ask the kids to let me have a turn. I also think that since the lady did not know me she probably thought that I was taking advantage of the other kids. These are the type of things that one cannot control, especially when there are other people involved. However, being aware of the surroundings can help avoid some bad experiences.

I learned something important that day and I put it to use very often. Not all rules are written down for people to follow. This is called common sense. Unfortunately, autistic people are not very good with common sense. The unwritten rules or common sense tell you how to act when there are others around. Most kids pick up common sense when they are growing up. No one has to tell them certain things because they can learn by watching others without thinking about it. However, autistic people like me need to be told. I needed to be told that it is expected that everyone takes turns spinning the web and that I did not need anyone's permission to spin it. If everybody was like me, there would be written rules posted everywhere.

My exercise for avoiding these situations used to be very tiring but it has gotten a lot easier. I can tell when I am nervous. My heart beats fast, too many pictures pop in my head and sometimes my hands shake. If I am alone or with people that I feel good with, I will do whatever makes me feel good. I can pace in a circle, hum out loud, rock back and forth, make facial movements, shake my hands or many other things I do that calm me down. However, if there are strangers around me, I can only do a few things. I have learned to hum inside my head. I try to block everything around me and hum a song I like. I also think of something funny that happened or imagine something nice. I have to be careful when I use my imagination because I had trouble in the past doing this. Remember the alien heads in Tae Kwon Do? I still laugh when I think about it.

I have noticed that what works really good for me is the silent humming and thinking about something nice like my dogs. If none of this works, then I take myself out of the situation. If there is a bathroom or a place I can go to until I feel better then I will go to it. When I feel better, I return to what I was doing. This works for me most of the time. There are situations when you cannot leave and those are really hard. Humming is what works for me. Therefore, using repetitive behaviors like humming, twirling, rocking back and forth or any other example is appropriate when they are done in the right place and time. Finding a behavior that is accepted in a public place that relaxes an autistic person is very important. It can soothe that person long enough to allow them to return to the activity they were doing without having to leave.

NOISES

People with autism feel better when they know what is about to happen. For this reason, sudden loud noises and smells can be shocking. Not being able to prepare for a sudden change can be unpleasant and can make me very anxious.

Many autistic children can become upset at the sight of balloons or fireworks. This is unfortunate because there are many times when balloons and fireworks are part of fun celebrations. For example, most birthday parties are decorated with beautiful balloons. There are also many restaurants that employ a clown-like person to go around the tables offering animal shaped balloons to the kids. I have also gone to several theme parks that have firework displays.

When it comes to balloons and fireworks, what may be fun and enjoyable to most children could be terrifying to most autistic kids. I lost count of how many birthday parties I went to but stayed only for a few seconds. The moment I noticed balloons I would cover my ears, drop off my gift and go home. I would spend days before the party wondering if there would be balloons there, how many, what shape and color and other things related to them. Then I would feel terrible days after the party because I left and had no fun.

I remember many restaurants where my family had to walk out after ordering the food once I saw a balloon person coming around the tables or if I saw a kid anywhere in the restaurant with a balloon. Finally, going to the theme parks and having to hide inside a restaurant while the firework displays are going on. Just like with the birthday parties, I would spend days before the trip to the theme parks thinking about the fireworks. Some of the things I wondered about were what colors and how many will there be, how long will the display last for and for how long after that will I smell the afterward smoke. My mind would become full of worries mixed in with the excitement of a fun trip.

It is very hard to plan some activities, especially when there are other people involved. Going out to eat, to the movies or to the parks is something that is usually done in groups of people. Ruining other people's fun makes me sad. I don't get scolded when these things happen but sometimes I feel that people were sad because of my fears. For this reason, I have learned to plan ahead with all this in mind. What I am trying to do with all this planning ahead is to avoid disappointment and feel less nervous.

Since these are things out of my control, there are limited things I can do when it comes to balloons and fireworks. The best thing is to find out as much as possible about the event. Knowing ahead of time makes me feel that I have some control. If there is a group gathering, we try to drive there in a separate car. I will not be able to play with other kids on the way there and back but it is more important to me to know that I can leave when I want and everyone else can stay. I find out if there will be things at the place that can upset me and if so, I can choose not to go. I have learned that I rather miss a magic show than spend the whole show being afraid while I expect the magician's balloon to pop or the loud explosion when the pigeon appears. I know which restaurants in my area do not have a balloon person and I rather eat there. When there is a chance to go to a new restaurant, we call ahead and ask or if there is no chance to call ahead, we ask the hostess what we need to know when we get there. Sometimes we are out of luck but luckily there is always a McDonalds or Burger King when everything else fails. Finally, all theme parks with fireworks display have a schedule they follow. I find out exactly at what time the display will take place and I am sure to be in a place where I cannot hear them such as a restaurant or inside a ride. I still feel nervous all day checking out the time, making sure I have plenty of time to hide, but I choose this option rather than miss the fun.

Most people do not understand all the planning that autistic people have to do just to try to make things enjoyable. Most humans take this for granted because their mind works in a different way. Most kids love the fireworks display and they don't need to keep their eyes on the clock, or plan, or be afraid. So, it is hard for others to understand how we feel. Maybe I can explain this better with another example that can allow people to understand how an autistic person can feel in a restaurant when surrounded by kids playing with their balloons.

I love snakes. All shapes, colors and sizes, especially the ones with beautiful patterns. I know that there are some that are poisonous which I will not touch. I like to touch their skin and hold them as long as I know that they are not dangerous. Imagine that a woman by the name of Rose is afraid of snakes. She walks into a restaurant with her family. After everyone orders their meal, she notices that an employee is going around the tables offering non-poisoning snakes, all shapes and colors, to the kids. Most of the kids at the restaurant are holding at least one snake, if not more. While the kids eat, they are either playing with them, placing them on the seat, table or the floor. Sometimes the snakes explode, making a loud noise and their bodies splatter all over the table. All this is happening while Rose is trying to enjoy her yummy food, keep a smile on her face and participate in conversations with the people around her.

Once everyone finishes dinner, Rose will probably be a little eager to go home where she feels out of danger because she knows there are no snakes there. Unfortunately, she will not be so calm when she finds out that from now on there is a big chance that next time she goes to a restaurant she may find these beautiful creatures all over the place. She has plenty of time to think about her next beautiful dinner experience and can imagine all the different snakes sliding up her chair until they get to the top of the table in order to accompany her while she enjoys her dinner.

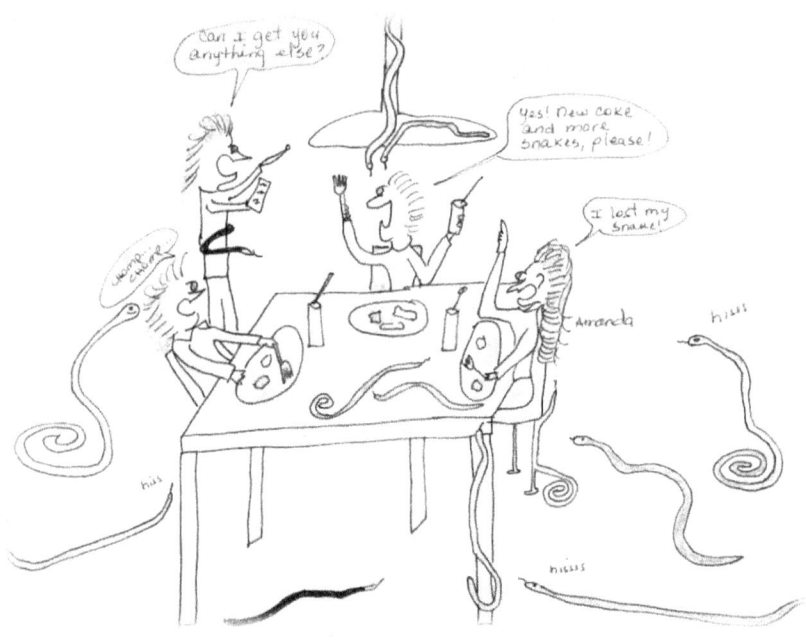

This made-up story about Rose would not be a problem for me if I was her but facing a couple of balloons is a big deal for me. Every time that I had a bad experience with balloons in a restaurant, the people around me try to help me but they don't really understand how I feel. Sometimes they give me advice that makes no sense to me. I know they mean well and they don't understand why their ideas do not work. People have told me in the past not to look at the balloons, to look away or to sit with my back to them. I wonder if a person who is afraid of snakes could enjoy their time in a restaurant seating with their backs to them knowing that the beautiful creatures are there sliding around.

I cannot control life outside my home, but I try to prepare for it. My exercises for noises and fireworks are simple but take a lot of repetition. I watch Youtube.com on the computer and there I look for videos to watch over and over. There are a lot of videos that have balloons and fireworks. I can watch them as many times as I want. First, I lower the volume all the way while I watch the video and when I feel comfortable, raise it a bit more. Autistics can be very sensitive to sounds, so I never raise it where it would hurt my ears but to a medium volume. This helps me get accustomed to the noise but not to the surprise. Once I memorize a video, I already know when the loud noise is coming and I am prepared for it. When I cannot predict when a sudden noise will come I cannot prepare and it will be unpleasant.

Everyone is surprised by a loud noise and they may scream but then they return to normal. This happens everywhere including the movies. The difference is that after people scream because they were surprised in a movie, they usually laugh and move on. It is harder for autistic people to react like that. We may sit there for the rest of the movie worried that there may be more loud noises and this can take away all the fun.   When everything else fails, I return to the simple ear covering. If I am at the movies and become surprised or scared by a loud noise, I first decide whether I want to stay or leave. If I chose to stay, I will probably cover my ears often but it helps to know I have the choice to leave.

In the past, I have chosen to stay at the movies where some kids had balloons in front of me. I was very nervous but the movie was exciting so I stayed. I spent the last half of the movie covering my ears just in case the balloons popped but the volume was loud enough where I could still hear what was going on. My ears were red afterwards from all the hard pressing I did. It makes me sad to know that a lot of people do not understand this and think that we may be impolite or brats.

ENERGY

Energy is great when you can get rid of it. It feels like millions of bubbles inside your body that keep popping releasing strength over and over. I call this having the "fasties". When I feel tired and slow, I say I have the "slowies". Energy is great because it helps you do things faster. However, it can be a problem when you have no way of getting rid of the fasties. This is true for everyone. Some people may have a lot or not much energy just because that is the way they are. I know that there are some medical conditions and diets that can affect energy levels, but I cannot talk about those because I do not know enough about it. I am referring to regular energy and what happens when you do not get rid of it.

Having a lot of energy cooped up inside can make a person nervous. I will talk later in more detail about anxiety but for now I just want to mention that not using energy can make a person anxious. There are positive and negative ways of using up energy. Anything that helps burning up energy is positive. Exercising or playing games can be fun. Unfortunately, not everyone likes to exercise or may have no one to play with. Participating in a sport is excellent because not only energy is being used but there is social interaction present. People, especially teenagers like me can become anxious or gain weight if they do not burn up their energy. Some people feel better eating when they are anxious.

Many autistic people like me have a high level of anxiety. If we do not learn how to use energy in a positive way, everything around us can be very hard. It would be very difficult to do any type of autistic exercise when I feel this energy cooped up and nowhere to go. I have been told by my family, teachers and friends that I have a lot of energy. For this reason, burning up the energy in a physical way is not hard for me.

I believe that it's very important to find a physical activity that the autistic person likes. Someone may enjoy something very much but not have the chance to do it. For example, someone that enjoys cycling but does not have a bicycle. We autistic are very simple people. We enjoy spending time doing simple things especially if there is repetition involved. The important thing is to find out the type of activity that the autistic person likes and if possible, facilitate things for them to do it.

Many years ago, I remember that I used to see an occupational therapist. Some of the things she had me do when I was with her were twirling, jumping around and getting small things with my hands because my visual motor coordination was not good. I remember she told my parents to help me find ways to burn a lot of energy because otherwise I would not be able to concentrate doing other things. She knew how much I loved to twirl around and told my parents to hang a special swing from one of our trees in the yard with a truck tire at the end of the swing. This was so that I could put my body through the tire and just swing for as long as I wanted. This happened about 10 years ago but I still remember I spent many hours playing with that swing. I am 15 years old now and still have a swing like that one.

I like biking, running, swimming and anything else that makes me move. I also enrolled in Tae Kwon Do and I go as often as I can. Sometimes, when my class ends but I still feel a lot of energy I ask the instructor for permission to stay for the next class. I have noticed that when I do a lot of exercise I sleep better at night and wake up with the fasties. The fasties help me get through the whole day without feeling tired and I do things quicker and happier.

I have also been told that I have a healthy appetite. I cannot think of anything I don't like. I remember very little before I was

2 years old but my mother tells me she always fed me all different types of food. I think this helped me to not be a picky eater today. I also like junk food but it is not my favorite. I can eat chocolate, cookies or chips but I rather eat a good piece of steak.

I mention food because I know other autistic kids like me that eat when they have a lot of energy. I think this is their way of burning up the energy but it can be bad when the food they eat is junk food. They are burning up energy because they are moving their body. It feels good because when a person eats they are moving their body in a pattern. Hand to plate, hand to mouth, swallow and start over again. This pattern can make us feel very good. Having healthy snacks can help. This can be tricky but not impossible. It is true that we do not like change. If you change my snacks, I will not like it. However, if there is nothing else to eat I will eventually snack on whatever is there. Here is an example of why I believe this to be true:

My dog Pipo has been with me for about a year. He came from another home where he was used to eating the type of food that they fed him. When he came to live with me he did not eat for the first two days. He was probably sad he got kicked out of his old home or did not like the food I gave him. He went without food for almost two days. At the end of the second day, his food bowl was empty. I am glad this happened because he learned to eat different foods. Today, when I go to the store for dog food I buy different brands with different choices of food. Pipo does not care anymore. As long as I feed him at the same time every day, he is happy with whatever I put on his bowl.

Parents of autistic teenagers like me may think that it's very hard to change our diets. I know someone that is like me and always wants to eat the same thing. If his parents don't please him, he gets very upset and refuses to eat anything at all. Anxiety takes place when the autistic person sees a different type of food and realizes that his pattern has been changed. The lack of control occurs when the pattern is changed and we are offered a different type of food that we were not expecting. We will most likely reject this type of change if it surprised us. But even with all these things against us, it is not impossible to change our diet as long as it is planned carefully and little by little. The person's likes and preferences have to be taken into account. Since patterns are something that most of us have in common, they can be used to make this change easier. Things like cutting food into squares, thin lines, or any other type of pattern helps. I eat little carrots which I decorate around the plate in circles. It looks orderly and it makes sense.

ANXIETY

There is good and bad energy. I call it positive energy when there is something good and exciting going on and something good will happen at the end. Negative energy is when I feel all this strength inside me and I know that at the end something bad may happen. When I feel anxious, I feel very tense with a lot of energy inside me. Many things can cause anyone to be nervous. Most of the time people know why they are nervous. Being excited, afraid, angry or worried about something can cause anxiety. People can deal with their anxiety in different ways.

Some of the ways that people deal with their anxiety is humming, whistling, tapping a pencil, exercising their bodies or breathing exercises. I know people who twirl their hair or call people on the cell phone and talk until their battery dies. These are usually accepted by others since it is not unusual to see someone doing any of these things. Autistic people become nervous too and have to deal with their anxiety as well. However, we have a tendency to deal with our anxiety displaying behaviors that can be seen by others as abnormal, funny or annoying. Flapping our arms, rocking or spinning can be very relaxing to us. I think that moving around somehow helps release some of that energy that can cause anxiety inside of us.

During science class with Mr. Bello, I learned that energy is the capacity for vigorous activity. When I feel anxious or tense, I feel that the best way to calm down is getting rid of all that energy inside me. Tapping a pencil or twirling my hair does not work fast enough. However, spinning is ideal. I also enjoy very much jumping on a little trampoline that I have in front of the television. The trampoline is great because I can jump for as long as I want, I can create my own patterns as I jump and it helps me to get rid of the "fasties". Unfortunately, if I am nervous, this is something I cannot do in a public place because people will be upset or laugh at me. This means that somehow, I would have to find a quick way that is accepted by regular people to get rid of the "fasties". This can be difficult because the circumstances in every case can be different so I cannot act the same way each time. If I don't think quickly, the anxiety can build up even more and make things worse.

In order to explain myself better, think for a moment that I am standing in front of my house and I see that a car runs over a puppy two houses away from mine. All the anxiety would make me want to run over as quickly as possible to see how the puppy is doing. Imagine now that society would not allow people to run no matter what. I would be forced to walk to where the puppy is. Meanwhile, my anxiety would grow more and more for not being allowed to run and because people would be staring at me. Frustration, anxiety and impotence are what we autistics may feel when we cannot calm down the way that helps us the most. However today I can understand a little better why some things cannot be done in public and I do whatever I can to find other ways that I can act.

I have a few favorite songs. I have learned to sing inside my head. Sometimes I sing so loud inside of me that I can barely hear what is going on around me. If I have a hard time, then I cover my ears and close my eyes so that I can sing louder inside my head. I try not to close my eyes because people will notice but will do it if there is no other way. The songs I like are all in YouTube, so I have seen the music videos. I have an excellent memory and I can remember most things with their pictures and sounds the exact way they happen. Singing or humming inside my head works better when I can picture the video as well and I relax faster that way. This is one of the ways that I use to calm down when I am in a public place. If I do it the right way, no one has to find out what I am doing and not only I get to calm down, but no one would have a reason to laugh at me.

GROOMING

Grooming is something that you learn to do daily as you grow up, I do not find it difficult to do because it is a repetitive action. Things like showering, brushing your teeth, wearing clean clothes, cleaning your ears and combing your hair are purely routine. Some people like to lay out their clothes the night before. An autistic person may not understand why these things are done daily, but since it is repetitive, may do them as a routine.

I understand the importance of being well groomed. One time I went to a place and walked past a man who had blue eyes and smelled really bad. His teeth were yellow and black and his hair was a mess. He was wearing blue jeans and a dirty yellow shirt and his fingernails were very dirty. He was talking to himself and what he said made no sense to me. I was not scared because I was not alone but I felt bad for him because there were people laughing at him. He was asking for money but no one wanted to get close to him. I pictured him with nice clothes, smelling nice and looking groomed. He was not ugly and looked a little like Santa Claus but skinnier. If he had been groomed, I think people would have given him money or at least they would have been nicer to him. I know that people will like you better if you are clean so remembering how I felt when I first saw the poor dirty man helped me understand how important it is to do daily grooming.

Grooming is something that high functioning autistics can learn especially if we are being taught using patterns. We can learn a little at a time and eventually do it without thinking. The steps to follow are always the same. The toothbrush is held in a certain way, once the toothpaste is applied, the movement to brush the teeth can be done in a pattern. Showering is similar. Once inside of the shower the same pattern is used to apply and rinse the soap. Combing the hair involves movements in the same pattern. This may sound easy but it can become very hard. If something fails everything else will follow. For example, if we run out of soap in the middle of the shower it will break the pattern. It's very important that the autistic person has access to all the things that are needed to complete the routine without complications. All of this depends on the level of functioning of the autistic person. Some may need to depend on others to make sure that everything is in order while others may be able to groom themselves. The first time I washed my hair all alone, I did not rinse all the shampoo out. I was in a rush to finish and thought no one would notice. When the hair finally dried, my head became so itchy that I had to go back and do it all over again. I learned to recognize through the touch of my fingers when there is no more shampoo left. We can do all of these things and more as long as we have someone" that is patient and willing to help us. The hardest part is to begin the training. Sometimes there are so many things involved that it seems like an impossible task to accomplish and impossible will be, if we never get started.

Autistic people may show difficulty when it comes to matching clothing. We may have a difficult time telling what colors match or clash. Remember that we are weak in social cues so it is difficult to be up to date in new styles and season colors. It would be logical for me to wear a shirt with squared patterns with pants that have lines. I know that people would laugh at me and compare me to a clown but it does not look strange to me. I have also seen people that are dressed in a way that I want to laugh but I understand that since I am what they call a minority, they are probably dressed correctly.

Not long ago I was watching television and saw a program where a princess was getting married. Many on the lady guests were wearing weird looking hats. Some were not that bad but others looked funny. I remember a specific one that looked like there was a huge bird with blue feathers sitting on a nest, which was the lady's head. I think that even if everybody was wearing a hat like that I would not be able to do the same. Just thinking that I have a huge bird nesting on my head would make me crack up just like I did in Tae Kwon Do with the alien heads. I rather not wear a hat like that.

There are a few things that I have learned when it comes to clothing. Because I cannot foresee every single possible occasion out there, I learn as I go and always ask for help when I feel lost. Watching television helps me see how people dress for different occasions. I have learned that it is acceptable to wear jeans and a t-shirt in most cases. However, special occasions like a wedding, birthday or religious activities may require more elegant clothing. Also, there are colors that are preferred at times such as black for a funeral or green for St. Patrick's Day. These things are learned when they are done time after time. Many times, dress codes do not make sense to me but I realize that this is one of those things that I have to go along with what is expected at the time.

As time goes by, I realize that I used to be a complete disaster when choosing my clothes but I also recognize that I have improved a lot in this area. There are still times where the clothes I wear do not make much sense to me but I understand that if I want to be accepted by society I have to dress the way they expect me to. I only hope that I never have to go to a Royal Wedding because no matter what, I will never wear a hat like the one with the blue bird on it.

SELF ESTEEM

I was not aware of many things related to autism until about a year ago when I found out that I am autistic. For this reason, I did not realize or understand many of the things that I realize today. Today I pay a lot more attention to things that are going on around me. In the past, even though I would not stare at people I would still notice when they were staring at me. I used to get very uncomfortable when people were staring because I did not know why they were doing it. My mother used to tell me that people would stare at me because I was beautiful. I did not believe that. After spending a little over a year learning more about autism and doing my exercises I think now that many times I was stared at because I was doing something that seemed odd to them. Perhaps I was rocking back and forth or hand flapping and this would make people look at me.

Thanks to the exercises that I have been doing, I have found other ways to feel comfortable around people and there are other things that I do now in public to calm me down that do not attract much attention.

I have learned that self-esteem is basically how you feel about yourself. The better that you feel about yourself, the better that your self-esteem will be. Having a high self-esteem allows you to do a lot of things without being afraid that you will fail or that people would laugh at you. There might be things that you are willing to do when no one is looking and you may be very good at them. However, the moment that there are people watching you, you may not want to give it a try for fear of failing. This can happen a lot to autistic people.

It is difficult to have a high self-esteem when you second guess everything you feel or do. Because we see things different than most people, we have the tendency to second-guess most things. For example, a person that is going to cross the street may wait at the corner for the pedestrian light to turn green. Once the light turns green, that person may cross without giving it a second thought and continue with his plans.

An autistic person may think of hundreds of questions on her mind before deciding to cross. Will all the cars stop on time? What if a car runs the light? What if the pedestrian light changes suddenly while I am in the middle of the street? Will there be other people crossing? Will I be the only one crossing? And other questions that are too many to mention here. It would not be uncommon for an autistic person to wait several change of lights before making the cross to the other side of the street. This way the autistic person has a chance to see and study the patterns that are going around the crossing. Did all the cars stop on time every occasion? Were there a lot of people waiting to cross? Did the pedestrian light change too fast for the people to make it across? The reason we autistics do these things is not to make a study of how pedestrians cross the street. We do this because we feel safer if we know what the patterns are so that we can make it safely to the other side. Once we feel confident making it across we will be more comfortable doing so. As you can imagine, it is very hard for us to have to a high self-esteem when we second-guessing everything we are about to do.

I have heard that the more you know, the more you realize how little you know. This is true in my case. For example, in the past I would not understand why people stared at me. This happens less today because I have become more aware of the things I do. Today I know that if I do hand flapping people will stare. If I feel the urge to do something that seems odd to other people, I have to spend the extra brain energy to try to stop it before I do it and find another way of feeling good without attracting attention. Sometimes I am successful but other times I am not. It is easier to catch it before it happens that to fix it after someone has noticed. I was not worried about stopping any behaviors before I became aware that I was autistic. So, the more I know, the more effort I make to try and make things "right". Things were easier in a way when I did not know all the things that I know today. The truth is that some time ago I would not spend so much time second-guessing everything I did but probably spent as much time wondering why things happened to me. I wish there was a pill that people could take to boost self-esteem but there is not. There are some things that I do alone or with others that I know that have helped my self-esteem.

First, I was given the homework to find out things that I am good at. This happened last year and I was having a hard time coming up with examples. Most of the examples I came up with were not very good but I learned that this happens when your self-esteem is low. I had a hard time seeing my strong qualities and did not give them much credit. Many times it takes someone else to point out the good qualities they see in you for you to become aware of them. Unfortunately, if your self-esteem is low you would have a hard time accepting the fact that you are good at something.

My mother always told me that I have a golden memory. I never paid much attention to that. She is always saying good things about me and sometimes I don't think that they are all true. I know that mothers say good things about their children so I thought that she was just being a mom. She used to point out things to show me how good my memory was but I still did not believe her. However, I did realize that I could remember a lot of things that most people would usually forget. Still, I never thought I had a special "gift" until one day it came clear to me.

When I don't want to hear something, I can shut a person off by thinking about something else but always try not to get caught. I usually do this when I am home or even at school with people that I know well because I feel safe and secure and I can disconnect my mind knowing that no one is going to hurt me. One of the ways that I distract myself from what is going on around me is by watching a movie in my mind.

I memorize things easily. I do not do this on purpose. All these things just become recorded in my head without me realizing. This happens not only with movies but also with anything that goes around me such as conversation between people or any other interactions between people or animals.

There is a great movie that I enjoy very much. I have seen it many times and know the movie by hard. It is called Ratatouille and it is about a rat that loves to cook. I enjoyed the movie so much the first time that I saw it that I bought it, so that I could watch it at home. I realized that it immediately recorded in my mind. This made me happy because this meant that I could watch it whenever I wanted without having to be in front of the television. At the beginning I had to close my eyes so that I could see the images better. If I kept my eyes open, it felt like if the lights were kept on at the movie theater while a movie is playing. I could still see the movie but it is a little foggy. Even with my eyes open I enjoyed my recordings a lot. I can rewind, pause or fast forward to whatever scene I want. When I think that someone's expression is funny, I pause it. I am careful when I do this because more than once I have cracked up out loud. If there is a section that is boring, I fast-forward to the next scene. It's like having an invisible remote control in my brain that controls the movie just like people do in real life with their remote control. Keep in mind that autistic people like me can usually be obsessive and like patterns and repetitions. Watching the movie in real life or in my mind for the second, third or fourth time allows a pattern to continue and I feel in control by being able to predict the end results. This is the reason why I don't mind for things to record in my head.

After a few times I learned to watch the movies with my eyes open and was able to make everything around me darker so that I could see the movie clearer. This happened because one day I was sitting on the table doing my math homework. The truth is that I was not doing homework but I was watching a movie in my head. My mother realized that my eyes were closed and asked me if I was falling asleep. At that moment I realized I had to find a way of enjoying my movies without anyone realizing so that they would not become upset with me for not doing what I was supposed to.

No one had ever realized that I could do that and I never told anyone because I thought that everyone could do the same. I just believed that the people doing it would be very careful not to get caught so that others would not realize when they were being ignored. One day was different than the others because I got caught.

My mother was upset at me and she was nagging while I watched Ratatouille on the television. My mother shut off the television and kept on nagging, and nagging and nagging some more. I continued to watch Ratatouille in my head. Since I already knew how to do this with my eyes open I thought it would be best so that I would not get caught. All of the sudden, the movie came to a hilarious part and I started to laugh out loud. My mother thought I was laughing at her and became furious. I had to tell her the truth about watching the movie.

My mother asked me to explain to her exactly what I was doing and why I was laughing in such a way. Sometimes she tells me that I laugh like a crazy cockroach. This confuses me because I have never seen a cockroach laughing so none of my mental pictures includes one. The fact is that I did not understand why my mother was so interested about my mental movies. She wanted to know everything in exact detail. I was confused because she was smiling and appeared to be surprised and happy. It made no sense to me. Up to that moment I still thought that everyone could do the same thing I was doing. My mother continued to ask more and more questions and sometimes when I answered her I thought it was funny because she would open her eyes wide like dinner plates and it seemed like they were going to explode. I had to explain to her in detail how I could see a whole movie with pictures, sounds, color and all, just like in the real screen, but in my head. She was so happy that she forgot what she was mad about. Then, she started asking about other movies, specific parts, what the dialog was, what color shirt or dress this person had...I thought that everybody could do what I was doing! I just thought that people could hide it better than me and that is why they were never caught.

It took a while for my mother to explain to me that most people were not able to do that because they did not have a memory like mine. She explained that some people could remember certain things but in a more general way. She also said that it's normal to remember certain details when they are important for somebody but it was not normal to remember all the details all the time.

Two good things happened that day. The first one is that my mother forgot why she was upset. The second one is that I finally discovered a strong quality that I had. It makes me feel good that I can memorize many things especially when people praise me for it. My mother does not write many things down any more but instead tells me to remember whatever she needs to be reminded of later on. Before we leave for the supermarket, she runs around the house looking for the things we need and yells them out loud so that my brain can record the items we need to buy.

It took me a while to complete the homework that I was given which was to find out what I was good at. I finally came up with real things like memorizing and doing physical things like biking, running or anything that has to do with burning energy. I also came up with eating a lot and not sleeping much but those don't count. However, knowing that I was good at something was the beginning for me to feel much better about myself. I am just very careful now not to get caught watching movies in my head when I am supposed to be doing something else like paying attention in class or doing homework.

The type of homework I was given can be hard to do for an autistic person. It is much easier when someone else is involved because they can give feedback and point out positive things that the autistic person may not be aware of. In my case it was my memory. Although I knew I had an ability to memorize things easily I did not see that as positive believing that everybody else could do the same. Biking, swimming or running did not strike me as any type of ability until someone pointed out to me that these types of activities help keep me healthy and allow me to "eat like a pig" without having to worry about gaining weight. There is something else and maybe more important that another person can do other than pointing out good qualities they see in you which is believing in you. I have a great example of something that happened to me last year.

I went to a Tae Kwon Do Tournament last year. I was scared, nervous and mortified about going to a strange place with strange people and competing in a huge auditorium. This meant I had to see new faces, get used to the new smells, lights and sounds and knowing that a lot of strangers were going to be staring at me probably while I was getting beaten up by another person. I am glad that there were other students that were going from my school and convinced me to go. Mr. Martin, one of the Tae Kwon Do instructors told me that he thought I would do well. I believed him because he's always right. Mr. and Mrs. Isaacs, the other two instructors at the Tae Kwon Do school, also told my mother that they thought I was ready to compete and would do well. Then I found out that the instructors were going to be there as well as other classmates so even though I was scared I decided to go. I made the right decision. There are times now that when I think that there is something that I cannot do I go to my room and touch the medal I won for sparring and it helps me think twice about not being able to do certain things.

I know that not every autistic person out there is lucky enough to have other people care for them and help them do these types of exercises with them. That is sad. However, I think it is even sadder that there are a lot of kids like me out there who do not do any type of exercises because the people that care for them do not know how well these can work. There are many times when I do not want to do an exercise because I want to do something else. I have been forced to do exercises at a time that I did not feel like it. I don't think that they work as well because I do not like to be forced and I usually get upset when this happens. However, it feels very good later on to see how the exercises have helped me and how much I have improved since I have been doing them.

There are other things that can help an autistic person improve their self-esteem. However, these depend mostly on other people. Feeling safe is one of them. If I feel threatened in any way I feel very unsure about what to do next. If anyone makes me feel safe when I feel scared there is a chance that I will not spend much time feeling insecure. Feeling that someone cares about you is very important. People that care about will not laugh at you, ridicule you or put you harm's way. It is easy to trust people that care about you and let them help you do things. In my case these people are family members and teachers.

I believe that it is very important for everyone to have someone to look up to, like a hero or a role model. It can be someone from television, a book or from real life. Having a role model gives people an idea of what kind of person they want to be like or what kind of things they want to do. Of course, it is great to be happy with yourself the way you are. However, if you see qualities that you admire in another person and it may improve qualities that you already have, the role model can serve as a guide for improvement.

My role model is my uncle Miguelangel Santimanzano, whom I call Tio Teto. I want to be like him in every way, except that he shaves his head sometimes and I don't want to do that. He is awesome in every way. His job is protecting the world from bad people. He is big and strong. He knows everything and everyone. Sometimes he disguises himself to do his job or just to play around. He has traveled all over the world and I just saw him doing an interview on television last week. All these things are awesome but they are nothing compared to the things he does for me. He always comes when I need him. He fixes my computer, finds my dogs when they escape and gets me amazing gifts. He gave me a horse named Bubbah, a police badge and a rifle so that I could be like him. He even helped my dad hang the tire swing and fixed my electric scooter...

Amanda   Tio Teto   Bubbah

Having a role model and hero like Tio Teto makes me feel safe because I know he will not let anyone harm me. It also makes me feel proud. I ask my mother to tell me stories about him that I don't know and some of those stories are great. I see how strong and daring he is and it makes me want to improve myself to be like him. He is not afraid of anything in this world and I believe he can do anything he sets out to do. Sometimes when I feel scared about anything, I ask myself what Tio Teto would do and it has helped me feel tough enough to do what I have to do.

It is also important to feel safe at school. Kids spend a lot of time in school and because of this we should feel safe in whatever school we go to. I go to a very good school. It is called Killian Oaks Academy and I have attended there since first grade. I went to a different school before I went here but I got kicked out. I remember that I went to that other school for about a year and was four or five years old. My parents got called in to see the principal and were told to look for a different school for me. My mother is very nice and told me that I had not been kicked out but that the principal was recommending a different school that could teach me better. Since I did not know that I was autistic until last year, I could not understand why they did not want me there. My mother told me that the teacher complained that I would jump on the desk and dance and that the rest of the kids would not be able to concentrate in class. Today, I think that I was probably so nervous that I just wanted to jump on the desk and twirl so that I could relax. The teacher probably thought I was dancing but I was just relaxing. At any rate, my mother still tells me that they did not kick me out but I know they did. From that moment on I started going to Killian Oaks Academy.

Even though I have not attended another school I can compare my school to others by watching the news, talking to family members who attend different schools and watching movies. There are a lot of things that happen in other schools that do not happen in mine. Fights, kids get picked on, teachers are mean or someone may come in shooting students.

When I am at school it reminds me of being at Disneyland. The teachers are always smiling. They speak in a very soft tone of voice and will explain things over and over as many times that are needed until the kids understand the lesson. They never get mad at you.

Best of all, Killian Oaks Academy has cameras all over the place. These cameras are inside and outside of the school, so even the field and parking lot are being watched. No one can get in and hurt the students. There is a huge white gate that only allows parents or special buses to come in to drop off and pick up the children.

Coach Bello stands in front of the school every morning and greets the students as they are being dropped off. In the afternoon he takes the students to their parents' car and is always making sure that everything is okay and that no strangers come into the school. Ms. Ricon is the principal of the school but behaves like everyone's mom. She kisses the students in the head when she sees them and speaks in a soft voice. I don't think that anyone is afraid of talking to her or asking her anything. My mother calls her the queen. This is because queens are the bosses of their homes and they always know what is best. My mother is the queen in my home but she said that while I am away at school Ms. Ricon is the queen and I must respect what she says. I like her a lot and it is not only because I have been there for so long. I see her treating other children and you can tell that she behaves like a mother to everyone. I also like her because she looks like a Barbie doll. Dr. Ricon is another principal. She is Ms. Ricon's daughter and she is also very pretty but she spends more time with the little kids. Sometimes Ms. Ricon and Dr. Ricon stand in front of the school in the morning and welcome the children kissing them on the head. It is really nice... just like Disneyland without balloons and fireworks.

I talk about my school for a very important reason. Most of autistic people may be insecure about different things. It is hard enough that we have to deal with a lot of things that most people don't have to deal with. I think that being in a school like mine has helped me feel more secure in many ways. It is peaceful knowing that I am safe and that there will be no strangers coming into school and doing harm to me. It is also very important the way that teachers behave and how they correct and teach the students. In all the time that I have been there I do not remember one time where I was yelled at or laughed at by any teachers. Because of this, most of the time I am not afraid to raise my hand and ask questions. Of course, my autism is always present but there are times that I feel it stronger than others. When I am at school I don't feel it's so strong because everyone there is very nice.

There is one more thing that I can think about that has helped me a lot when it comes to self-esteem. Sometimes I see a psychologist. Her name is Dr. Shelley Slapion- Foote but I call her Dr. Shelley. She is very nice and very funny. She usually asks me how things are going and she lets me talk about anything I want. She always reminds me that I am a very important person and that my wishes have a lot of weight. She also tells me that I have a lot of potential and that I am a lot more intelligent than other people may think. It feels very good to know that you can talk to somebody about anything you want and you will not get into any trouble. I have never gotten into trouble but it just feels good to know that there is someone there in case I need her. I think that my self esteem has improved just by knowing that someone else is there for me.

I think that I have improved a lot this past year. One thing is for someone to tell you how good you are doing but it feels a lot better when you can see it for yourself. I know that all autistic kids can be different but we may also have a lot of things in common like in the way we act, feel, interpret things and think. Some of the exercises that work for me may not help all the autistic people in the world. However, there are a lot of things that we all have in common and these are the things I have written about. I hope that some of my exercises can help another person like me live a better life.

My final tip for anyone who wants to help an autistic person improve their self esteem is to remind them how much you care about them as often as you can. You can never do this enough or too many times. Sometimes we learn better if you show us what you are trying to say and if we make a mistake, encourage us to do better next time. Words can be confusing many times but a smile can go a long way. Be patient... we eventually learn to get it. When we get it, let us know you noticed.

For more information, visit **AutisticMe.org**

LEGAL NOTICE AND DISCLAIMER

www.ingramcontent.com/pod-product-compliance
Lightning Source LLC
Chambersburg PA
CBHW072338290526
45794CB00002B/921